VEGAN KETO

70 Healthy & Delicious Low-Carb Recipes

Marian Lee

Table Of Contents

SMOOTHIES & SHAKES 128

INTRODUCTION

This book is meant for those who wants to lead a healthy life by following a ketogenic vegan diet.

A ketogenic diet is low in carbohydrates and high fat. Usually, most of this fat will be derived from animal products. This is a big conflict with veganism, however, which does not use any animal products at all.

However, it *is* possible to create a vegan keto diet! This is achieved by using plant based foods that are rich in natural fats, such as avocado, nuts, some vegetable and nut oils, and more.

In this book, we have put together 70 delicious, healthy and easy-to-follow recipes that combine natural ingredients with some of the lowest amounts of carbs and highest amounts of fat. Many recipes use seeds, tofu or tempeh to provide a good balance of protein as well.

Carbohydrates are not totally eliminated in every recipe, but they represent a very small percentage of your meal when they *are* included.

The recipes are divided into ten different sections, to make it easier for you to browse through. Enjoy!

BREAKFAST

We all know that breakfast is the most important meal of the day. The recipes in this session will help you start your day with a healthy, substantial and delicious meal.

1. Keto Toasted Coconut Flakes with Almond Milk

This is a delicious meal to start your day with. The toasted coconut flakes are a great substitute for regular cereals, which are usually high in carbs and sugars.

Your body will benefit from the good fats in the coconut flakes and almond milk. Plus, you will feel full but light. You can toast the coconut in a big batch and keep it in an airtight container in the cupboard, ready to use at any time.

Yield: 5 servings
Prep Time: 15 minutes
Cooking Time 5 minutes

Ingredients:

- 1 lb. flaked coconut
- 1 tbsp. ground cinnamon
- 1/2 cup unsweetened almond milk
- 1 tbsp. dried cranberries
- 2 medium to large strawberries - sliced
- 1 sheet of baking paper

- 1 tsp. coconut oil

Preparation:

1. Preheat oven to 350F.
2. Line a baking tray with a sheet of baking paper. Grease the paper with coconut oil.
3. Pour the coconut flakes over the baking paper.
4. When the oven reaches the temperature, put the flakes in the oven and bake for five minutes. Keep an eye on the flakes the whole time as you do not want them to burn.
5. Shuffle the flakes around and keep baking until they are a little golden and lightly toasted.
6. Take the flakes out of the oven and sprinkle with cinnamon. Taste and if you like you can add more cinnamon.
7. Put 1 cup of the coconut flakes into a bowl. Sprinkle with the cranberries and add the unsweetened Almond milk.
8. Add the strawberries for extra freshness and enjoy your healthy breakfast!

2. Vanilla - Almond Chia Breakfast Pudding

Chia seeds are an excellent source of antioxidants, omega-3s, calcium and fiber. The seeds were one of the staples of the ancient Mayas and Aztecs because of their nutritional density.

By adding fruit to this deliciously creamy pudding, you will benefit from an incredibly nourishing breakfast. You can easily double up the amount of the ingredients and keep your pudding refrigerated for up to 5 days.

Yield: 2 servings
Prep Time: 5 minutes
Soaking Time: 1-8 hours

Ingredients:

- 2 cups unsweetened almond milk
- 1/2 cup chia seed (they enlarge when soaking)
- 1/2 vanilla pod
- 1-2 tbsp. raw honey
- Seasonal fruit of your choice (blueberries, strawberries, raspberries etc...)
- Almonds for topping

Preparation:

1. Put the almond milk, chia seeds, vanilla pod and honey into a large bowl.
2. Mix well until all ingredients are combined and the

mixture begins to thicken.

3. Cover the mixture and put in the fridge to rest overnight. If you do not have time, refrigerate for at least one hour. However, it tastes better if soaked overnight.
4. Take out of the refrigerator and stir well before serving.
5. If the mixture becomes too thick, you can add some water to loosen it up.
6. Top with the almonds and some fresh fruit of your choice.

3. Keto Cinnamon Crunchy Squares

This is another delicious alternative to regular cereals. The chia seeds will give you the right amount of energy to start your day, and the combination of banana, coconut and cinnamon flavors will give your nutritious breakfast a great taste.

Yield: 8 servings
Prep Time: 10 minutes
Cooking Time: 25 minutes

Ingredients:

- 1 cup of coconut flakes
- 1/2 cup of sunflower seeds
- 1/4 cup of chia seeds
- 1 tbsp. cinnamon powder
- Pinch of sea salt
- 1/4 cup raw honey
- 1/4 cup mashed banana

To serve:

- 1/2 cup of almond or coconut milk
- Seasonal fruit of your choice

Preparation:

1. Preheat the oven at 325F.

2. Put the coconut flakes, sunflower seeds, chia seeds, cinnamon and sea salt in a blender or food processor.
3. Pulse until the mixture becomes flour.
4. Place the flour into a mixing bowl, add the raw honey and mashed banana.
5. Blend well together to create dough.
6. Pour the mixture onto a sheet of baking paper and cover with another sheet of baking paper.
7. With a rolling pin, roll the mixture to form a rectangle approximately 8"x 10" and 1/4" thick.
8. Remove the top sheet and cut the dough into squares approximately 1/2"x 1/2".
9. Place the baking paper and the dough squares on a baking tray and put in the oven.
10. Bake for 20-25 minutes until the squares are dark brown.
11. Serve the crunchy squares with either almond or coconut milk, and top with seasonal fruit of your choice.

4. Breakfast Smoothie Bowl

Why not start the day with a filling smoothie bowl? This specific smoothie bowl is a great source of good fats thanks to the avocado and coconut milk.
This high fat and low sugar smoothie will make you feel full light and full of energy, ready to take on the day ahead with a spring in your step.

Yield: 1 large bowl (or 2 small bowls)
Prep Time: 10 minutes or less
Cooking Time: None

Ingredients:

- 1 cup creamy coconut milk
- 1/2 soft avocado
- 1/2 vanilla pod or 5 drops vanilla essence
- 1 tbsp. cocoa powder
- 1 tsp. cinnamon (optional)
- Some ice cubes (optional)
- Almonds, strawberry, blueberries or raspberries for topping

Preparation:

1. Add all ingredients into a blender and mix until smooth.
2. Pour the smoothie into a bowl and top with the almonds and fresh berries.

5. High-Protein Hemp Seed Porridge

Hemp seeds are a great source of protein. They are also high in omega 3 and omega 6 fatty acids, and low in carbs. Plus, they add a nutty, slightly sweet touch and a crunchy texture to your porridge. This makes the perfect breakfast for a cold or rainy day.

Yield: 1 large serving
Prep Time: 25 minutes
Cooking Time: 15 minutes

Ingredients:

- 1 cup almond milk
- 1/4 cup hemp seeds (outer shell removed)
- 1 tbsp. flax-seed meal
- 1 tbsp. almond butter
- 1 tsp. cinnamon

For topping:

- Almonds
- 1 tsp. raw honey (optional)

Preparation:

1. Put the almond milk in a saucepan over low heat and bring to simmer.
2. When simmering, add half of the flax-seed meal, half of

the hemp seeds and cinnamon.

3. Stir the mixture and continue to simmer on low heat for 10 minutes while stirring from time to time.
4. Make sure the mixture does not stick to the saucepan.
5. Turn the heat off and add the rest of the ingredients while stirring.
6. Leave to cool down for a couple of minutes.
7. Pour the porridge into a bowl and top with the almonds and raw honey.

6. Low-Carb Chia and Hemp Seeds Porridge

This is another winter warmer breakfast. The combination of chia and hemp seeds will boost your energy and provide your body with a good amount of fatty acids.

Yield: 1 large bowl
Prep time: 5-10 minutes
Cooking Time: 10 minutes or less

Ingredients:

- 2 tbsp. black chia seeds
- 2 tbsp. hemp seeds (outer shell removed)
- 1/2 vanilla pod
- 1 tbsp. shredded almonds
- 1/2 cup coconut milk

For topping:

- Handful of blueberries
- 2 large strawberries - sliced

Preparation:

1. Combine all ingredients in a saucepan and mix well.
2. Let the mixture stand for 5 minutes until the chia seeds assume a jelly-like appearance.
3. Put on the stove top at very low heat.
4. Warm up the mixture until bubbles appear.

5. Pour the porridge into a bowl and top with the blueberries and strawberries.

7. Keto Breakfast Bread

This bread recipe is actually very low in carbs. It does not use any flour and the main ingredient is almond butter which provides a great amount of good fat. You can store the bread in the refrigerator wrapped in a paper towel and sealed in a plastic bag. It will last up to one week or so.

This bread is delicious served with a vegan yogurt and topped with blueberries or strawberries.

Yield: 12 servings
Prep Time: 15 minutes
Cooking time: 15 minutes or less

Ingredients:

- 1/2 cup creamy roasted almond butter
- 1/2 cup unsweetened apple sauce
- 2 tbsp. raw honey
- 1/4 tsp. vanilla stevia
- 1/4 tsp. sea salt
- 1 tsp. baking soda
- 1 tbsp. ground cinnamon
- 1 tbsp. coconut oil

Preparation:

1. Preheat oven to 325F.
2. Place the almond butter in a large bowl and mix with a hand blender until creamy.

3. Mix in the applesauce, honey, and stevia.
4. Add salt, baking soda, and cinnamon.
5. Use the hand blender again to mix all ingredients until they are well combined.
6. Grease an 8"x 8" baking tray with the coconut oil.
7. Transfer the batter into the baking tray and bake in the oven for 12-15 minutes until golden on top.
8. Serve with vegan yoghurt and top with blueberries or strawberries.

8. Quinoa Breakfast Bowl

With this super-fast breakfast recipe, you will benefit from the excellent properties of quinoa. This very popular health food is very high in protein, gluten-free and it contains nine essential amino acids.

On top of that, quinoa is very nutritious and high in fiber. It is delicious cold, or you can warm it up slightly on the stove or microwave. This great energetic breakfast is the perfect kickstart to a busy day ahead.

Yield: 1 serving
Prep Time: 5 minutes
Cooking Time: 1 minute

Ingredients:

- 1/2 cup plain cooked quinoa
- 1/3 cup unsweetened almond milk
- 1 tbsp. almond butter

For topping:

- 1/2 cup fresh blueberries (you can use frozen blueberries as well)
- 1 tsp. cinnamon

Preparation:

1. Combine the quinoa, almond milk and almond butter in

a bowl.

2. Mix well together until you have a creamy mixture.
3. Add blueberries for toppings and sprinkle with cinnamon.
4. If you wish to have your breakfast warm, place in the microwave or stove top before topping with fruit.

9. Mix Seeds and Nuts Breakfast Bars

These nutritious breakfast bars are packed with protein and fiber thanks to the combination of seeds and nuts. Nuts are also a great choice for your daily intake of good fats.

You can make a big batch of bars and store them. They are perfect to grab a breakfast on the go if you don't have much time. You can store the bars for up to a week in an airtight container in the fridge.

Yield: 1 serving
Prep Time: 5 minutes
Cooking Time: 15 minutes

Ingredients:

- 1 cup desiccated coconut
- 1/2 cup hemp seeds - shells removed
- 1/2 cup sesame seeds
- 1/2 cup pumpkin seeds
- 1 and a half cups mixed nuts - crushed (almonds, walnuts, cashew, macadamia)
- 1 tbsp. cinnamon
- 1/2 cup dried cranberries
- 1/2 cup almond butter
- 1 tbsp. raw honey
- 1 vanilla pod

Preparation:

1. Preheat oven to 350F.
2. Combine the desiccated coconut, seeds, nuts, cranberries and cinnamon in a large bowl.
3. Place the almond butter and raw honey in a saucepan and melt on the stove on a medium heat.
4. Once the butter and honey are well combined, remove from the heat and add the vanilla pod.
5. Stir the mixture gently.
6. Add the content of the bowl into the saucepan and continue to stir until all ingredients are well combined.
7. If the mixture does not stick together, add a small amount of water to help it to stick better.
8. Take a brownie tin and line it with baking paper.
9. Move the compost to the brownie tin and press down so to form a flat and even layer.
10. Bake in the oven for approximately 15 minutes or until golden brown.
11. Take out of the oven and leave to cool completely before cutting. If you cut while still hot, the bars will crumble.
12. Cut into 12 bars. You can enjoy right away or store them for later.

SOUPS

Soups are the ultimate comfort food. They are the perfect warm meal on a cold day, and a simple meal to put together when time is an issue. You can make almost anything into a soup to be added as part of a healthy low-carb diet.

Soups can be full of healthy ingredients, and can provide you the right amount of nutrients needed to maintain a balanced vegan keto diet. We have put together some recipes using only the most low-carb vegetables to stick to a keto regime.

10. Broccoli Bisque with a Twist

This is a very simple recipe that combines broccoli as a very low carb vegetable with a high-fat vegetable like avocado. The added nuts are another great source of good fat and are also full of protein. This soup is a true combination of flavors and goodness, perfect for a quick lunch or dinner.

Yield: 2 servings
Prep Time: 20 minutes (excluding soaking)
Cooking Time: 15 minutes

Ingredients:

- 8 oz. fresh broccoli
- 2 ½ cups of water
- 1 cup raw cashew nuts - soaked and drained
- 1/2 clove of garlic

- 1 small soft avocado
- Juice of 1 lime or lemon
- Salt & Pepper to taste
- 1 tbsp. olive oil (optional)

Preparation:

1. Put the raw cashew nuts into a bowl, cover and leave to soak 6-8 hours or overnight.
2. Pour the water into a saucepan and bring to the boil.
3. Wash and split broccoli removing the hard parts of the stems but keeping most of them.
4. Once the water is boiling, add the broccoli and lightly boil until tender.
5. Drain the broccoli and save the water for later.
6. Drain and rinse the cashews.
7. Combine the cashews, broccoli, avocado and the water to a blender and blend at high speed until smooth and creamy.
8. Pour the mixture into a saucepan and warm up on a low heat while stirring occasionally until bubbles start forming.
9. If the mixture is too thick you can add a little bit of water.
10. Take off the heat, add lemon juice and salt & pepper to taste. Stir and taste.
11. You can adjust salt & pepper if needed or add more lemon to taste.
12. Pour your bisque into two bowls and garnish with some cashews and a drizzle of olive oil.

11. Cream of Spinach Soup

This is another excellent soup that is high in protein and good fat and low in carbs. It is very filling and nutritious and can be served as a light meal.

Yield: 4-6 servings
Prep Time: 30 minutes (not including soaking time)
Cooking Time: 30 minutes

Ingredients:

- 1 tbsp. olive oil
- 2 cloves of garlic - chopped
- 3.5 oz. white onion - sliced
- 1 oz. celery - diced
- 5 oz. green beans - diced
- 0.4 oz. parsley - finely chopped
- 3 oz. spinach
- 4 cups vegetable broth
- 1.2 oz. raw almonds - soaked
- Salt & Pepper to taste

Preparation:

1. Put the raw almonds in a bowl, cover and soak overnight.
2. In a large saucepan heat the olive oil over a medium heat.
3. Add the onion and sauté for 5 minutes until translucent.

4. Add the garlic, celery, green beans, a pinch of salt and sauté for another 5 minutes.
5. Add the vegetable broth and stir. Turn the heat to high, cover the pot and bring to boil. When the soup starts boiling, reduce the heat to low and simmer for 10 minutes.
6. Add the spinach and simmer for an additional 10 minutes.
7. Remove the saucepan from the heat and leave it to cool.
8. Drain the almonds and add them to the soup.
9. When the soup has cooled down a little, pour it in batches into a blender and blend on high speed for approximately 40 seconds until smooth and creamy. Blend longer if necessary.
10. You can return the soup to the saucepan and warm up or you can eat it straight away. Both ways it will taste delicious.
11. Add some ground black and serve.

12. Green Cauliflower Soup

The trick with soup is to keep it simple. Something as basic as cauliflower can make a deliciously creamy and tasty low carb vegan-friendly soup. The extra olive oil will add the good fats and a Mediterranean flavor perfect for a starter.

Yield: 8 servings
Prep Time: 25 minutes
Cooking Time: 25 minutes

Ingredients:

- 1 tbsp. extra virgin olive oil
- 1 medium white onion - chopped
- 3 cloves of garlic - chopped
- 3 lb. cauliflower (florets and stems) - cut into chunky pieces
- 5 cups of water
- 1/2 fresh parsley - roughly chopped
- 2 oz. green beans - chopped
- 1 oz. green beets - roughly chopped
- Salt & Pepper to taste
- Juice of 1/2 lemon

Preparation:

1. Heat the oil in a large saucepan over a medium heat.
2. Add onion and let it cook for approximately 5 minutes until translucent and soft.

3. Add garlic and stir. Add a pinch of salt and let it cook for a further 2-3 minute until garlic becomes golden or lightly tanned. Make sure not to burn the garlic.
4. Add cauliflower and stir. Pour in the water until it covers the cauliflower. Stir again.
5. Cover the pot and bring to boil over a high heat.
6. When the soup starts boiling, bring the heat to low and simmer gently for about 10 minutes or until the cauliflower is tender.
7. Add all your greens, stir and let simmer for another 3-5 minutes.
8. Take the soup off the heat, add the chopped parsley.
9. Let the soup cool for about 10 minutes.
10. Puree the soup with a blender until very smooth and creamy. If the soup is too thick for your taste you can add a little bit of water.
11. Return the soup to a low heat and warm up until bubbles form.
12. Take off the stove, add lemon juice, salt, and pepper to taste and stir.
13. Garnish with parsley and a drizzle of olive oil. Serve immediately.

13. Winter Italian Minestrone

Minestrone is the ultimate "cozy soup". It's tasty, filling and it provides your body with most of the proteins and minerals needed for a healthy diet. It is delicious hot on a cold winter day, or at room temperature on a warm summer day. You can make a big batch and store it in the fridge for up to 5 days, or freeze it for few months.

Yields: 8 servings
Prep Time: 25 minutes
Cooking Time: 45 minutes

Ingredients:

- 2 tbsp. coconut oil
- 1/2 cup white onion - diced
- 2 cloves of garlic - chopped
- 3 carrots - chopped
- 1 cup of mushrooms - chopped
- 2 courgettes - chopped
- 3 oz. broccoli - florets halved and stems chopped
- 1/2 cup green beans - chopped
- 2 large tomatoes - chopped
- 3 oz. cabbage
- 5 cups of water
- 1 tbsp. olive oil
- Juice of 1 lemon
- 1/2 cup parsley
- Salt & pepper to taste

Preparation:

1. Wash and prep all your veggies.
2. In a large saucepan, heat the coconut oil on a medium heat.
3. Add onion, stir, and cook for approximately 5 minutes, until tender.
4. Stir in the garlic and cook for another 2 minutes.
5. Add carrots, mushrooms, cabbage, tomatoes, and a pinch of salt. Stir well so that the veggies get the flavour from the onion and garlic
6. Add water, stir gently and bring to boil.
7. Cover, lower the heat to low and let simmer for 25 minutes. Stir occasionally.
8. Add broccoli, zucchini, and green beans and cook for another 10 minutes.
9. Take off the heat. Add parsley, lemon juice, olive oil and freshly ground black pepper. If needed adjust salt to taste. Let your minestrone rest for 5 minutes before serving.

14. Indian-Style Green Pepper, Courgettes, and Spinach Soup

This is a deliciously exotic low carb soup with a kick — thanks to the added Indian spices. It is another one of those soups that you can make a big batch of, and either keep in the refrigerator for few days or freeze for a longer time. The coconut milk will make this soup deliciously creamy. Yum!

Yield: 4-5 servings
Prep Time: 20 minutes
Cooking Time: 45 minutes

Ingredients:

- 1 small white onion - chopped
- 2 cloves of garlic - chopped
- 2 tbsp. coconut oil
- 1 tbsp. mild curry powder
- 3 medium size green peppers - chopped in large pieces
- 3 large courgettes - chopped into 1/2-inch round pieces
- 8 oz. spinach - roughly chopped
- 1 large tomato - chopped
- 2 tsp. tomato paste
- 1 can coconut milk
- 1 cup of water
- Juice of 2 limes
- 1/2 cup of coriander
- Salt & Pepper to taste

Preparation:

1. Heath the coconut oil in a large saucepan on a medium heat.
2. Add the onion and cook approximately 5 minutes, until tender and translucent.
3. Add garlic, stir and cook for another 2-3 minutes until garlic takes on a nice tanned colour.
4. Stir in the curry powder and cook for 2 minutes, until fragrant.
5. Add the chopped tomatoes and tomato paste and a pinch of salt. Mash all ingredients together and cook for another 5 minutes until you have a creamy paste.
6. Add coconut milk and water. Stir and bring to boil.
7. Cover the pot, lower the heat to low and simmer for 5 minutes.
8. Add green peppers and courgettes. Turn the heat up to medium-high and bring to boil again.
9. Turn the heat down to low and simmer for 25 minutes.
10. Take off the heat, add lime juice, coriander and freshly ground black pepper. Add salt to taste if necessary.
11. Let your soup rest for 5 minutes and serve.

SALADS

Salads are some of the easiest, fresher and healthiest meals you can make. You can have salad as a light lunch, an entree or a side dish. You can add anything to it, like avocado, nuts, seeds, etc., and you can be sure to have a delicious and nutritious option ready to go.

15. Cucumber Salad

Cucumber is one of the veggies with the lowest amount of carbs. You can pair it with almost anything. For this particular recipe, we combined it with avocado and nuts for that extra fatty kick. You can make a large portion and have it as a light lunch or divide it into small portions for a delicious side dish.

Yield: 4 side servings
Prep Time: 15 minutes or less
Cooking Time: None

Ingredients:

- 2 large cucumbers - peeled, deseeded and cut into julienne
- 1 cup cherry tomatoes - cut into quarters
- 1 small soft avocado - sliced
- 1 clove of garlic - minced
- 1/2 cup olives - chopped
- 1/2 cup walnuts - chopped

<u>For the Dressing:</u>

- 2 tbsp. extra virgin olive oil
- 1 tsp. grainy mustard
- Juice of 2 lemons
- 1/2 tsp. salt
- 1 tsp. freshly ground black pepper
- 1/4 cup fresh parsley - roughly chopped

Preparation:

1. In a large bowl combine the cucumber, cherry tomatoes, avocado, walnuts, olives and minced garlic.
2. In a small bowl put the lemon juice, mustard, salt, and pepper. Whisk together.
3. Slowly add olive oil while whisking. Keep whisking until obtaining a creamy dressing. If the dressing is too thick, you can add more olive oil or few drops of water.
4. Pour dressing onto salad and gently toss together. Serve and enjoy.

16. Cauliflower Summer Salad

This is another low-carb salad to add freshness and taste to your hot summer days. We added nuts for a good protein intake, and extra virgin olive oil for the good fat intake.

Yield: 5 servings
Prep Time: 15 minutes
Cooking Time: None

Ingredients:

- 1/2 head of iceberg lettuce - thinly sliced
- 3.5 oz. cauliflower florets - raw and cut into small pieces
- 1 medium carrot - cut into julienne strips
- 1 cup button mushrooms - peeled and thinly sliced
- 1 cup cherry tomatoes - halved
- 2 oz. fennel - thinly sliced
- 1/2 cup macadamia nuts - crushed

For the Dressing:

- 2 tbsp. extra virgin olive oil
- Juice of 1 lemon
- 1 tsp. balsamic vinegar
- Salt and Pepper to taste

Preparation:

1. Combine all the vegetables in a large bowl.
2. In a separate small bowl whisk in together all ingredients for the dressing.
3. Pour the dressing onto the salad, toss gently until evenly coated and serve.

17. Fennel and Green Beans Pesto Salad

Some vegetables are better eaten raw. As an added bonus, raw food is quick and easy to make, saving you time for other things.

Yields: 3-4 servings
Prep Time: 15 minutes
Cooking Time: None

Ingredients:

- 1 lb. green beans - chopped into medium pieces
- 2 fennels - outer removed and thinly sliced
- 1 large tomato - diced
- 1/2 cup cashew nuts - chopped

For Pesto:

- 2 cups basil leaves
- 2 tbsp. extra virgin olive oil
- 1 clove garlic -
- 1 tbsp. lemon juice
- Salt & Pepper to taste

Procedure:

1. Prepare pesto first.
2. Put the basil and garlic in a food processor or blender.
3. Process or blend until the basil and garlic are

completely chopped.

4. Add the olive oil in a stream while the processor or blender is running.

5. Add the lemon juice, salt, and pepper and mix again. At this point, you should have a nice smooth runny paste. Taste your pesto and adjust for salt and pepper if necessary.

6. Take a large bowl and add all the salad ingredients.

7. Pour the pesto over the salad and gently toss to combine.

8. Your salad is ready to serve.

18. Baby Spinach, Mushrooms and Nuts Salad

If you love salads but are a bit bored of using lettuce, baby spinach is a great alternative to use. The young crunchy leaves are a great source of iron. Pair it with the avocado dressing and nuts and you will have a delicious low-carb, high fat salad.

Yield: 2 servings
Prep Time: 15 minutes
Cooking Time 10 minutes

Ingredients:

- 2 cups of baby spinach – roughly chopped
- 1 cup button mushrooms – sliced
- 1 cup cherry tomatoes – halved
- 1 clove of garlic – chopped
- 1 tbsp. extra virgin olive oil
- Salt & Pepper to taste
- 2 tbsp. water
- ½ cup of walnuts – roughly chopped

For the Dressing:

- ½ soft avocado
- 2 tbsp. extra virgin olive oil
- Juice of 1 large lemon
- Salt & Pepper to taste

Preparation:

1. Put the oil in a frying pan and preheat over a medium-high heat.
2. When the oil is hot, throw in the garlic and cook for 1 minute.
3. Add the mushrooms, salt and pepper and cook until the mushrooms release their water and become small.
4. Add water and keep cooking for another minute.
5. Set aside and leave it to cool down. Drain the mushrooms and keep the cooking juice.
6. In a large bowl place the baby spinach, cherry tomatoes and walnuts.
7. Put the avocado, olive oil, lemon juice, salt and pepper in a blender. Blend for about 30 seconds until you have a smooth and creamy dressing. If the dressing is too thick you can add some drops of water and blend again.
8. Taste and adjust for salt and pepper if necessary.
9. Pour the dressing onto the salad and gently toss before serving.

19. Roasted Vegetables, Tofu & Pumpkin Seeds Salad

For this delicious salad, we have combined a choice of low-carb vegetables with fats from extra virgin olive oil and olives, and we have added the extra proteins of pumpkin seeds and tofu. Everything combined together makes this salad a perfect filling choice for a light lunch or dinner, packed with all the right nutrients.

Yield: 4 servings
Prep Time: 10 minutes
Cooking Time: 40 minutes

Ingredients:

- 1 pack extra firm tofu – cut into bite size cubes approximately 1" size
- ½ head of broccoli – cut florets into approximately 2" size, discard the stems
- ½ head cauliflower – cut florets into approximately 1" size, discard the stems
- 1 cup white button mushrooms – halved
- 1 eggplant – cut into approximately 2" chunks
- Extra virgin olive oil
- ¼ cup black olives – chopped
- ¼ cup pumpkin seeds
- Salt & Pepper to taste

Preparation:

1. Preheat oven to 400F.
2. Drain the tofu and pat with a paper towel to absorb as much water as possible.
3. Cut tofu into cubes.
4. Drizzle 1 tablespoon of extra virgin olive oil on a baking tray. Place the tofu on the baking tray and shake gently so that the tofu gets evenly coated with oil.
5. When the oven reaches temperature, place the tofu on the upper rack and start roasting.
6. Place all the pre-cut vegetable on another baking tray, add 2 tablespoons of extra virgin olive oil, a pinch of salt and freshly ground black pepper and toss gently to evenly coat.
7. Place the baking tray in the oven on the lower rack.
8. Roast for approximately 30 minutes, checking the vegetables from time to time.
9. Remove vegetables from the oven and set aside to cool.
10. If some of the vegetables are not completely cooked, remove the cooked through vegetable and leave the rest in the oven.
11. Take the tofu out of the oven and flip over on the tray.
12. Turn up the oven to 450F.
13. Place the tofu back in the oven and roast for another 10-15 minutes. Make sure the tofu gets a nice brown colour on both sides.
14. The tofu should be brown and crispy on the outside and soft on the inside.
15. Remove from oven and let it cool down for approximately 5 minutes.
16. Add the pumpkin seeds, olives and tofu to the roasted vegetables.
17. As an option you can add some fresh parsley and lemon juice.
18. Gently toss together and serve.

20. Kale, Avocado & Grilled Tempeh Salad

Tempeh is an excellent source of vegan protein that originates from Indonesia. It is very healthy, while also being versatile; you can have it deep fried, pan fried, grilled, steamed, and so on.

It is delicious in soups and curries, in particular. We paired it with raw Kale for an extra crunchy, low-carb salad, and added the fat of avocado and a good amount of extra virgin olive oil for your high intake of fats.

Yield: 4 servings
Prep Time: 10 minutes
Cooking Time: 10 minutes or less

Ingredients:

- 8 oz. pack of tempeh – cut into slices approximately 0.2" thick
- 1 tbsp. coconut oil
- 8 oz. black kale – rib removed from each stalk
- 4 oz. radishes – very thinly sliced
- 1 cup cherry tomatoes - halved
- 1 soft avocado - diced

For the Dressing:

- 3 tbsp. extra virgin olive oil
- 1 tsp. Dijon mustard
- Juice of 2 lemons

- 1 tsp. apple cider vinegar
- Salt & Pepper to taste

Preparation:

1. Preheat grill to medium-high.
2. Oil the grill rack using the coconut oil.
3. Place tempeh on the rack and grill until lightly charred, approximately 3-5 minutes each side.
4. Set tempeh aside.
5. Stack the kale leaves in small batches and cut into thin slices.
6. In a large salad bowl place the kale, radishes, avocado and cherry tomatoes.
7. Crumble the grilled tempeh over the top.
8. In a small bowl whisk dressing ingredients together until creamy.
9. Pour the dressing over the salad, toss gently and serve,

LUNCH

As most of us are leading rather busy lifestyles these days, we cannot afford to spend much time preparing lunch. However, we still want to keep our lunch healthy and free from any kind of junk food. With our quick and easy-to-follow lunch recipes, you can be assured that you will be able to enjoy a healthy low-carb keto dish that does not require much preparation.

21. Curry Cauliflower Rice

This recipe can sound a little bit misleading, since rice should not be part of a low carb diet. In fact, there isn't actually any rice in this recipe. Cauliflower is what gives this dish a texture similar to rice, while still keeping the carbs very low.

Yields: 4 servings
Prep Time: 10 minutes
Cooking Time: 10 minutes

Ingredients:

- 1 head cauliflower
- 1 clove of garlic - chopped
- 1 tbsp. coconut cream
- 2 tbsp. extra virgin olive oil
- 1 tbsp. mild curry powder
- 1/8 tsp. cinnamon
- ½ cup cashew nuts - halved
- ½ tsp. salt
- Black pepper to taste

- ½ cup coriander – roughly chopped
- Juice of ½ lemon

Preparation:

1. Separate the cauliflower florets from the stem.
2. Chop the florets into approximately 2 inch pieces.
3. Place half of the cauliflower into a food processor. Pulse with 1 second intervals until the cauliflower pieces look like grains of rice.
4. Move the processed cauliflower into a bowl.
5. Repeat the process with the other half of cauliflower.
6. Heat the extra virgin olive oil in a large saucepan over a medium heat.
7. When the oil is hot, add the curry powder, cinnamon, and fry for approximately 1 minute.
8. Add the cauliflower and cashew nuts and stir until coated with the curry powder
9. Add salt and coconut cream and cook for 5-8 minutes or until tender.
10. Remove from the heat; add coriander, black pepper and lemon juice.
11. Let it rest for couple minutes and serve.

22. Zucchini Noodles with Vegan Cheese Sauce

Some of us might be on a vegan diet for reasons that are different from the vegan ethical beliefs, and we might miss the texture or flavor of a cheese sauce. This easy-to -make low carb zucchini recipe will fix your cravings for a cheesy sauce, and will give your body a good dose of healthy fats thanks to the extra virgin olive oil.

Yield: 2 servings
Prep Time: 15 minutes
Cooking Time: None

Ingredients:

- 3 medium zucchini – sliced very thin with a mandolin slicer or basic grater
- ½ cup walnuts – chopped
- Black pepper

For the Cheesy Sauce:

- 2 tbsp. extra virgin olive oil
- Juice of 1 small lemon
- 2 tbsp. nutritional yeast
- Pinch of salt

Preparation:

1. Combine all ingredients for the cheesy sauce and mix together.
2. Place the zucchini noodles and walnuts into a bowl.
3. Pour the cheesy sauce onto the zucchini noodles and top with ground black pepper.
4. Toss gently and serve.

23. Asian Style Green Beans with Walnut Butter

This incredibly quick and simple recipe combines the high fat of the walnut butter and coconut oil with the low-carb green beans. This dish can be enjoyed on its own as a quick lunch or served as a side.

Yield: 3-4 servings
Prep Time: 10 minutes
Cooking Time: 10 minutes

Ingredients:

- 1 ½ lb. green beans – trimmed
- 2 tbsp. walnut butter
- 2 tbsp. tamari
- 2 tbsp. avocado oil
- 1 tbsp. water
- 1 tbsp. coconut oil
- 1 clove of garlic – minced
- 1 tsp. fresh ginger – minced
- ½ tsp crushed black pepper

Preparation:

1. Steam the green beans for approximately 5 minutes or until just tender.
2. Rinse under very cold water, drain and set aside.
3. In a small ball mix together the walnut butter, tamari,

avocado oil and water and set aside.

4. Heat the coconut oil in a large wok or frying pan over a medium-high heat.
5. Add the beans and stir-fry for 30-40 seconds.
6. Remove the beans from the pan or wok and set aside.
7. In the same wok used for the beans, add the garlic, ginger and crushed black pepper.
8. Stir-fry for 15 seconds.
9. Add the beans to the wok and sir-fry again for 30 seconds.
10. Add the walnut mixture previously prepared and stir-fry until the beans are all coated with the mixture.
11. Serve immediately.

24. Tangy Brussel Sprouts

Brussel sprouts are not very popular among some people. If you find the right recipe, however, they can be just as delicious as any other veggie. On top of that, they contain a low amount of carbohydrates, and they are a great source of vitamin A, B and C, as well as potassium. Follow this simple recipe, and you will be pleasantly surprised.

Yield: 4 servings
Prep Time: 10 minutes
Cooking Time: 20 minutes or less

Ingredients:

- 1 ½ lb. Brussel sprouts – discard stem and cut into quarters
- 2 tbsp. coconut oil
- Juice of 1 lime
- Zest of 1 lime - grated
- ½ inch piece of ginger – peeled and minced
- 1 clove of garlic – minced
- 1 tbsp. tamari
- ½ cup cashew nuts.
- ½ tbsp. raw honey
- Salt & Pepper to taste

Preparation:

1. Preheat oven to 350F.

2. Line a baking tray with baking paper.
3. In a large place the coconut oil and melt in the microwave for 15-30 seconds. If you do not have a microwave, you can melt it by placing the bowl on top of a saucepan containing boiling water.
4. When the coconut oil is melted, whisk in the zest and juice of lime, ginger, raw honey, salt, pepper, garlic, and tamari. Whisk until ingredients are all combined together.
5. Toss the Brussel sprouts into the coconut oil mixture and add the cashew nuts.
6. Arrange the sprouts on the baking paper on a single layer.
7. Put in the oven and roast for 8 minutes. Remove from oven, stir and place back into oven for a further 8 minutes
8. Take out of the oven add another sprinkle of ground black pepper and serve.

25. Colourful Walnut Tacos

These tacos are a great alternative to the meat tacos. The walnuts mixed with the rest of the ingredients will give a meat-like texture packed with proteins. The corn flour tortillas are replaced by lettuce leaves as a low-carb option.

Yield: 2 servings
Prep Time: 15 minutes
Cooking Time: None
Soaking Time: overnight

Ingredients:

For the Tacos:

- 2 cups walnuts – soaked overnight
- 2 tbsp. ground cumin
- 1 tbsp. extra virgin olive oil
- 1 tsp. paprika
- Salt
- ¼ tsp. cayenne pepper
- Lettuce leaves as many as needed

For the Guacamole:

- 1 large soft avocado or 2 small
- Juice of 2 limes
- Salt & Pepper

For the Pico de Gallo:

- 2 large tomatoes – chopped in very small square pieces
- ¼ red onion – chopped in very small square pieces
- Juice of 2 limes
- Salt & Pepper
- 1 tsp. extra virgin olive oil
- ½ cup coriander – roughly chopped

Preparation:

1. Soak the walnuts overnight.
2. Put all ingredients for the tacos, except for the lettuce leaves, in a food processor.
3. Process until the mixture looks like the texture of minced meat.
4. Set aside.
5. In a small ball place the avocado, salt and pepper, and lemon juice and mash until smooth.
6. In another bowl, place the ingredients for the Pico de Gallo and mix well together.
7. Scoop the taco mix into the lettuce leaves and serve with guacamole and Pico de Gallo on the side.

26. Sautéed Brussel Sprouts with Radicchio and Almonds

Here we have another favorite with Brussel sprouts. This time we paired it with radicchio. Radicchio is a great source of vitamins B, C and K, and is high in antioxidants.

Yield: 3-4 servings
Prep Time: 10 minutes
Cooking Time: 20-25 minutes

Ingredients:

- 1 ½ lb. Brussel sprouts – stem removed and sliced in half
- 2 heads Radicchio – roughly chopped
- 3 tbsp. avocado oil
- ¼ cup Almonds – shaved
- ¼ cup of red onion – diced
- 2 cloves of garlic – minced
- Salt & Pepper

Preparation:

1. Heat 2 tablespoons of avocado oil in a large frying pan or wok over medium-high heat.
2. Add the Brussel sprouts and cook them for about 10 minutes. Stir occasionally.
3. In the meantime, heat the remaining avocado oil in a small frying pan over medium heat.

4. Add the red onion and sauté for 4-5 minutes until translucent.
5. Add the almonds and garlic.
6. Cook for an additional 4-5 minutes until they become lightly brown. Remove from the heat as you do not want them to burn.
7. Back to the sprouts. When they start to brown, add the Radicchio and continue to cook until the Radicchio becomes tender.
8. Remove from the heat and add the toasted almond mixture.
9. Add salt and pepper, toss everything gently and serve while still hot.

27. Tofu, Broccoli and Green Pepper Stir-Fry

This is another winner lunch, as it is made in no time, and ticks all the necessary boxes for a healthy vegan Keto diet. It is low in carbs and high in proteins and good fats. If you like, you could replace the tofu with tempeh instead.

Yield: 2 servings
Prep Time: 10 minutes
Cooking Time: 25 minutes

Ingredients:

- 6 oz. firm tofu
- 2 tbsp. cashew nuts
- 3 tbsp. coconut oil
- ½ tbsp. raw honey
- 2 cloves of garlic - minced
- 1 inch piece of ginger – minced
- 4 spring onions
- ½ of broccoli cut into florets
- ½ green pepper - sliced
- Juice of 2 limes
- 2 tbsp. tamari
- ½ cup coriander – roughly chopped

Preparation:

1. Pace a frying pan or a wok on the stove over high heat.
2. Add the cashew nuts and toss around the wok or pan

for approximately 1 minute or until golden.
3. Remove from the heat and place into a bowl.
4. Dry the tofu with paper towel then cut it into bite size cubes.
5. Place the tofu into a bowl and sprinkle with a small pinch of salt and about ½ teaspoon of crushed black pepper.
6. Put 2 tablespoons of coconut oil into the wok or pan and place over medium- high heat.
7. When the oil is hot, fry the tofu until golden and crispy.
8. Spoon the tofu out of the pan and set aside on a sheet of paper towel to absorb the extra oil.
9. Return the empty pan to the stove on medium-high heat.
10. Add 1 tablespoon of coconut oil, then add the garlic, ginger, spring onions, and stir-fry until the garlic takes on a slightly golden colour.
11. Add the broccoli, green pepper, salt and stir-fry for 4 minutes. Add the raw honey, lime juice and tamari and stir for another 30 seconds.
12. Add the coriander and remove from the heat.
13. Serve immediately with lime wedges on the side.

28. Almond & Coconut Asparagus

Asparagus are some of the most delicious veggies around, and they can go well with a wide range of other ingredients. The bright green part of the asparagus is packed with vitamins, minerals and fiber to help your body stay healthy.

Yield: 4 servings
Prep Time: 10 minutes
Cooking Time: 15 minutes

Ingredients:

- 1 ½ lb. asparagus – remove the white part at the back
- 1 tbsp. coconut oil
- ½ cup white onion – diced
- 1 clove of garlic - chopped
- 2 tbsp. sliced almonds
- 1 tsp. paprika
- ½ tsp. red chili flakes
- Pinch of salt
- 1 cup coconut milk
- Juice of 1 lime
- ½ cup fresh coriander – roughly chopped

Preparation:

- Heat the oil in a large frying pan over medium heat.
- Add the almonds and fry until they become to brown. Be careful not to burn them.

- Move the almonds to a plate and set aside.
- Return the empty pan to the heat; add onion, garlic, paprika, chili flakes and a pinch of salt.
- Cook until the onion becomes soft and stats to brown.
- Add the coconut milk and stir well.
- Add the asparagus and stir well.
- Bring to the boil, cover and reduce heat to low.
- Simmer until the asparagus are tender, approximately 5 minutes. If you like the asparagus softer let them simmer for longer.
- When you are happy with the tenderness of the asparagus, remove the lid and continue cooking until the sauce becomes a little thicker. If you like it runnier, you can remove from heat now.
- Once removed from heat, add lime juice and coriander.
- Stir once more and serve.

29. Sautéed Quick Lunch Veggies

This mix tasty veggies must be one of the quickest and easiest recipes to prepare. In 30 minutes, you will have a delicious and healthy lunch full of protein and good fats. You will feel full, energetic and ready for the second part of your busy day.

Yield: 2-3 servings
Prep Time: 15 minutes
Cooking Time: 15 minutes

Ingredients:

- 2 tbsp. extra virgin olive oil
- ½ small red onion – finely chopped
- 1 green pepper – diced
- 2 cups broccoli florets – cut into small pieces
- 2 cups cauliflower florets – cut into small pieces
- 2 cups spinach – roughly chopped
- 1 cup mushrooms – chopped
- 2 cloves of garlic – finely chopped
- 1 cup Brussels sprouts – stems cut off and cut into quarters
- Salt & Pepper
- ½ cup fresh parsley – roughly chopped

Preparation:

1. Heat the oil over medium heat in a large frying pan.
2. Add the onions and cook until translucent.

3. Add the garlic and cook for another 2 minutes approximately.
4. Add all your vegetables except for the spinach and sauté for approximately 10 minutes. Stir occasionally.
5. Add the spinach, salt and pepper.
6. Stir well together and cook for another 5 minutes. If you like your vegetables softer, cook for extra 10 minutes in total.
7. Take off the heat and add fresh parsley.
8. Serve immediately.

30. Stir-Fry Vegetables & Bamboo Shots with Crispy Tempeh

Here is another spot-on lunch recipe that can be made in less than 30 minutes. We combined two incredibly low-carb veggies with a rich protein source in tempeh. In addition to being low in carbohydrates, bamboo shoots are also very rich in iron, potassium, minerals and some important vitamins such as A, B6 and E.

Yield: 4 servings
Prep Time: 10 minutes
Cooking Time: 10 minutes

Ingredients:

- 8 oz. pack Tempe – cut into small strips
- 3 oz. canned bamboo shoots – julienned
- ½ white onion – chopped
- 1 inch piece of ginger – thinly sliced
- 2 cloves of garlic – thinly sliced
- 1 small courgette – julienned
- 5 button mushrooms – sliced
- ½ lb. green beans – cut into 1 inch pieces
- 3 tbsp. of water
- 2 tbsp. tamari
- 1 tsp. raw honey
- Juice of 2 limes
- Salt & Pepper
- 4 tbsp. coconut oil
- ½ cup fresh coriander – roughly chopped

Preparation:

1. Put 2 tablespoons of coconut oil in a wok or large frying pan and heat over a medium heat.
2. Add the tempeh and fry until brown and crispy.
3. Remove from the pan and set aside on some paper towel.
4. Return the pan to the stove. Add 2 tablespoon of coconut oil and heat over medium-high heat.
5. Add garlic and ginger and stir-fry until lightly golden.
6. Add the rest of the vegetable and a pinch of salt and stir fry for 3-5 minutes.
7. Add honey, tamari, lime juice and water and stir fry for another minute.
8. Remove from heat, add fresh coriander and serve with crispy tempeh sprinkled on top.

DINNER

For some people, dinner is the main meal of the day. The family gets to dine together after a busy day and spend some quality time together while enjoying delicious, healthy food. The great thing about spending time cooking dinner is that if you have leftovers, you can easily have them for lunch the next day.

31. Cauliflower and Cashew Nuts Indian Style

Cauliflower is a very popular veggie among chefs because of its great versatile texture and because of its ability to absorb other flavors. Cashew nuts add proteins and fat to this exotic flavorsome dish.

Yield: 3-4 servings
Prep Time: 15 minutes
Cooking Time: 35 minutes

Ingredients:

- 1 very large cauliflower – florets and stems chopped into medium pieces
- 3 tbsp. coconut oil
- 1 tsp. cumin seeds
- 1 small handful curry leaves
- ½ tsp. fennel seeds
- 4 cardamom pods
- ½ white onion - finely chopped

- 5 cloves of garlic – minced
- 1 inch piece of ginger – minced
- 2 medium tomatoes –chopped
- ½ cup Cashew nuts
- 1 tbsp. coriander powder
- ½ tsp. turmeric powder
- ½ tsp. Garam Masala
- ½ cup coconut cream
- ¼ cup of water
- Fresh Coriander – roughly chopped
- Salt & Pepper

Preparation:

1. Heat the coconut oil in a large pot over medium heat.
2. Add cardamom pods, cumin and fennel seeds.
3. When the seeds start splattering add the onion and curry leaves.
4. Fry for a couple of minutes then add a pinch of salt, stir and keep cooking until the onion is translucent (approximately 5 minutes).
5. Add ginger and garlic and cook for another 2-3 minutes.
6. Add the spices and stir-fry for a couple minutes, until fragrant.
7. Add the chopped tomatoes, stir and cook for 5 minutes.
8. When the mixture becomes mushy add the cauliflower and cashew nuts. Stir well together.
9. Add the water and coconut cream. Mix well.
10. Bring to boil. Cover the pot and cook over medium heat for about 12-15 minutes depending how tender you like your cauliflower.
11. Remove from the heat. Add salt and pepper to taste,

fresh coriander and stir.

12. Cover and let it rest for 5 minutes before serving.

32. Grilled Avocado Stuffed with Broccoli and Tofu

This might sound like a strange recipe, because when we think of avocado we think of guacamole and salads. The flavor and simplicity of this dish will surprise you.

Yield: 4 servings
Prep Time: 40 minutes
Cooking Time: 10-15 minutes

Ingredients:

- ¼ cup extra virgin olive oil
- 1 tbsp. grainy mustard
- 1 clove of garlic – chopped
- Pinch of chilli flakes
- ½ tsp. ground cumin
- ½ cup of fresh parsley – roughly chopped
- Juice of 1 lemon
- Zest of ½ lemon – grated
- Salt & Pepper to taste
- 1 pack of extra firm or firm tofu – cut into ½ inch cubes
- 2 stalks of broccoli – remove and discard stems, cut florets into medium pieces
- 3 ripe avocados – need to be firm

Preparation:

1. Put the olive oil, mustard, garlic, chilli flakes, lemon

Juice, lemon zest, salt, pepper and cumin in a small bowl. Whisk all ingredients together to make a marinade mix then set aside.

2. Put the broccoli and tofu into a large dish and pour the marinade over.
3. Cover the dish and refrigerate for at least 30 minutes.
4. While the broccoli and tofu are marinading, preheat the grill to high.
5. Cut the avocado in halves and remove the pits
6. Brush the inside of the avocados with some olive oil and sprinkle with salt and pepper and set aside.
7. Place the broccoli and tofu in a grilling tray under the grill and grill until tender and with brown bits. Make sure you do not place them too close to the grill or they will burn.
8. When ready remove from the grill, add fresh parsley and gently toss.
9. Place the avocado halves under the grill until the start colouring.
10. Spoon the broccoli and tofu into the avocado halves, drizzle a little bit of olive oil on top and serve.

33. Eggplant and Coconut Milk Curry with Cauliflower "Rice"

Eggplant is an excellent low-carb vegetable with a unique texture and very distinguished flavor. It is very nutritious and a good source of dietary fiber. It pairs very well with the cauliflower rice. You can use the cauliflower rice raw, or you can cook it in the microwave for 5 minutes (or steam it on the stove).

Yield: 4 servings
Prep Time: 10 minutes
Cooking Time: 25 minutes

Ingredients:

- 1 lb. eggplant – skin on and cut into 1 inch pieces
- ½ white onion – diced
- 1 inch piece of ginger – minced
- 2 cloves of garlic – minced
- ½ cup Cashew nuts
- 3 tbsp. coconut oil
- 1 cup coconut milk
- 1 tbsp. mild curry powder
- Salt & Pepper to taste
- ½ cup fresh coriander – roughly chopped

For the Cauliflower "Rice":

- 1 large cauliflower – stem removed, florets cut into medium pieces

Preparation:

1. Start by making the cauliflower "rice".
2. Put the cauliflower florets in a food processor with a grating blade. A regular blade will also do.
3. Pulse until the cauliflower looks like rice. Make sure not to overdo or you will end up with a mash.
4. If you do not have a food processor, you can use a hand grater.
5. Set the rice aside.
6. Put the coconut oil in a large frying pan and heat over medium-high heat.
7. When the oil is hot, add the eggplant and cook for approximately 5 minutes until the eggplant is seared. Stir occasionally.
8. Add onion, garlic, ginger and cook until soft while stirring.
9. You can add a little bit more oil if necessary as the eggplant tends to absorb most of it.
10. Add curry powder and stir well.
11. After about 1 minute add cashew nuts, coconut milk, black pepper and a pinch of salt.
12. Simmer for about 5 minutes or until the sauce is slightly reduced.
13. Take off the heat and add fresh coriander. Stir gently.
14. Serve over the cauliflower "rice".

34. Pan-Seared Tempeh Steak with Roasted Cabbage and Walnuts

This recipe contains everything your body needs for the perfect low-carb, high-fat regime by combining the tempeh, cabbage, nuts and a good amount of extra virgin olive oil.

Yield: 4 servings
Prep Time: 1 hour
Cooking Time: 40 minutes

Ingredients:

For the Pan-Seared Tempeh:

- 1 lb. tempeh – cut into 3 ½ inch long by 3/8 inch thick slices
- ¼ cup water
- 1 garlic clove – minced
- 1 tsp. dried oregano
- ¼ tsp. pepper flakes
- ¾ cup extra virgin olive oil
- 6 tbsp. red wine vinegar

For the Roasted Cabbage:

- 1 medium head of green cabbage – cut into 8 wedges and core trimmed.
- Juice of 1 lemon
- 2 tbsp. extra virgin olive oil
- Salt & Pepper

Preparation:

1. Preheat oven to 450F.
2. In a plastic sealable bag combine the water, red wine vinegar, garlic, oregano and pepper flakes. Add tempeh, press out the air and seal the bag.
3. Toss the bag to completely coat the tempeh with the marinade.
4. If you do not have a sealable bag you can use a mixing ball and cover it with cling film.
5. Refrigerate your tempeh for 1 hour. You can marinade for longer if you have time.
6. Place wedges on a roasting tray. Arrange them in a single layer.
7. Sprinkle walnuts on top.
8. In a small bowl, whisk together the extra virgin olive oil and lemon juice.
9. Pour the mixture on top of the cabbage and season with salt and pepper to taste.
10. Gently toss the wedges to completely coat with the mixture.
11. Roast each side of the cabbage for approximately 15 minutes until nicely browned.
12. After 1 hour, remove tempeh from the marinade.
13. Pat tempeh dry with a piece of paper towel.
14. Take a large skillet or frying pan and heat the olive oil over medium heat.
15. When the oil is hot add tempeh and cook for about 2-4 minutes until golden brown.
16. Turn tempeh on the other side and reduce heat. Cook for another 2-4 minutes.
17. Remove from the heat and move tempeh onto a sheet of

paper towel over a plate.

18. Serve on a plate with the cabbage.
19. You can top with a drizzle of extra virgin olive oil.

35. Scrambled Tofu with Guacamole

If you do not have much time to cook dinner, but still want to benefit from healthy ingredients, this is a very easy and quick recipe to whip up a tasty main course in no time. This is such a delish and light meal that can also be made for a savory breakfast.

Yield: 4 servings
Prep Time: 10 minutes
Cooking Time: 10 minutes

Ingredients:

- ½ white onion – diced
- 1 stick of celery – diced
- 1 courgette – diced
- 1 green capsicum - diced
- 2 cloves garlic - minced
- 1 inch piece of ginger – minced
- 1 lb. firm tofu
- ½ bunch fresh coriander – roughly chop leaves and finely chop stalks
- 2 tbsp. coconut oil
- 1 tbsp. ground turmeric
- 1 tbsp. ground cumin
- 3 tbsp. tamari sauce
- Ground Black Pepper
- ½ cup pumpkin seeds

For Guacamole:

- 2 large soft avocados
- Juice of 2 large limes or lemons
- Salt & Pepper
- 1 large tomato - diced

Preparation:

1. Drain tofu and pat dry with paper towel.
2. Crumble tofu.
3. Prepare the guacamole. Cut avocados in half and remove pits.
4. Scoop avocados into a bowl. Add lime juice, salt and pepper and mash.
5. Add the diced tomato and stir to combine. Set aside.
6. Heat the coconut oil in a deep frying pan over medium-low heat.
7. Add all the diced vegetables to the frying pan.
8. Stir continuously and cook until tender.
9. Add garlic, ginger and coriander stalks.
10. Stir and cook for another minute.
11. Add all the spices and stir to coat.
12. Add tofu and stir until tofu is evenly coated with spices.
13. Remove from the heat.
14. Stir in coriander and tamari sauce. Sprinkle with ground black pepper.
15. Serve topped with lots of avocado and garnish with pumpkin seeds.

36. Cauliflower Couscous with Roasted Vegetables

This super healthy dish benefits from the low carb content of cauliflower couscous instead of using the real couscous, which is much higher in carbs. We have added almonds for extra crunchiness and nuttiness, and pared it with juicy veggies roasted in plenty of extra virgin olive oil.

Yield: 4 servings
Prep Time: 30 minutes
Cooking Time: 35 minutes

Ingredients:

For the Cauliflower Couscous:

- 1 medium cauliflower – cut into large florets – stems removed
- 1 cup fresh parsley – roughly chopped
- ½ cup roasted almonds – crushed

For the Roasted Vegetables:

- 2 eggplants – skin on and cut into 1 inch pieces
- 2 green capsicums – diced into 1 inch pieces
- 2 cups of button mushrooms – cut into halves
- 1 broccoli head – florets cut into halves
- 3 tbsp. olive oil
- 2 cloves garlic – crushed
- ½ cup fresh coriander – roughly chopped

- Salt & Pepper

Preparation:

1. Preheat oven to 392F.
2. Fill a saucepan with water and bring to boil.
3. When water boils drop cauliflowers in. Cook for 3 minutes.
4. Drain and cool under cold water. Drain well.
5. Place the florets into a food processor; add parsley and pulse to obtain a fine crumb.
6. Move the crumbs into a bowl and add roasted almonds. Combine together and set aside.
7. Place vegetables on a baking tray.
8. Add garlic, thyme, extra virgin olive oil, salt and pepper to taste and toss well together.
9. When oven is hot place in oven and roast for 30 minutes.
10. Remove from the oven and serve over the cauliflower couscous.
11. Top with a drizzle of extra virgin olive oil and fresh coriander.

37. Tempeh Curry Laksa Style with Kelp Noodles

This exotic recipe is inspired by the Laksa dishes, originally from Malaysia and Indonesia. We used coconut milk for a creamy texture, kelp noodles for their low carb content, and tempeh for its delicious nutty flavor and high amount of protein.

Yield: 4 servings
Prep Time: 10-15 minutes
Cooking Time: 30 minutes

Ingredients:

- ½ lb. Tempeh – cut into 1 inch cubes
- Coconut oil
- 1 small chili – deseeded and finely sliced
- 2 cloves of garlic – minced
- 1 inch piece of ginger – minced
- 1/ white onion - finely chopped
- 1 medium eggplant – cut into 1 inch pieces
- ¼ cup Laksa paste
- 6 curry leaves
- 1 ½ cup vegetable stock
- 1 can coconut milk
- 2 x 11 oz. packs kelp noodles
- 2/3 cup fresh coriander – roughly chopped
- Salt & Pepper
- Juice of 1 lime

To Serve:

- 1/2 cup Cashew nuts
- ½ cup coriander – finely chopped
- 1 spring onion – finely sliced
- Lime wedges

Preparation:

1. Heat ¼ cup of coconut oil in a frying pan over medium-high heat.
2. Cook tempeh in 2 separate batches until golden brown.
3. Remove from the pan and set aside on a sheet of paper towel.
4. Place a big tablespoon of coconut oil in a saucepan and place over medium heat.
5. Add the onion, chili, garlic, ginger, curry leaves and Laksa paste.
6. Stir well and cook for 4 minutes.
7. Add the eggplant and a pinch of salt. Stir well until eggplant is coated with the spices and cook for another 4 minutes. If the pan is too dry, add an extra spoon of coconut oil.
8. Add vegetable stock, coconut milk and a sprinkle of ground black pepper.
9. Bring to boil and lover the heat to low.
10. Cover the pan and simmer for 15 minutes. Stir occasionally.
11. Remove the pot from the heat. Stir in the chopped coriander, fried tempeh and lime juice.
12. Remove kelp noodle from their package and rinse with

cold water and cut them in half with a kitchen scissor.
13. Add the noodles to the curry pot and stir gently.
14. Divide the curry into bowls and top with fresh coriander, spring onions and cashew nuts.
15. Serve hot with extra lime wedges.

38. Walnut Stuffed Eggplant with Rocket Salad

We brought the eggplant back for another great recipe. The walnuts will add a kind of "meaty" texture, plus lots of protein and healthy fats to this easy-to-make meal.

Yield: 2 servings
Prep Time: 15-20 minutes
Cooking Time: 40 minutes

Ingredients:

- 1 large long eggplant – cut in half lengthwise
- 1 cup walnuts
- 2 medium-large ripe tomatoes - chopped
- 2 cloves of garlic – chopped
- ½ red onion – diced
- 2 tbsp. extra virgin olive oil
- Salt & Pepper to taste
- ½ cup fresh parsley – roughly chopped

For the Salad:

- 7 oz. rocket leaves
- 1 cup cherry tomatoes – cut into halves
- 1 tbsp. extra virgin olive oil
- 1 tsp. balsamic vinegar
- Juice of ½ lemon
- Salt & Pepper

Preparation:

1. Preheat oven to 356F.
2. Place walnuts in a food processor and pulse until the texture resembles minced meat. Set Aside.
3. Place the eggplant on a baking tray and with a knife cut the centre flesh into diagonal crisscross.
4. Drizzle with extra virgin olive oil and sprinkle with salt and pepper.
5. When oven is hot, put the eggplant in the oven and bake for approximately 20 minutes.
6. Leave to cool for few minutes, then scoop out the flesh and place into a bowl.
7. Heat the oil in a frying pan over medium heat. Add garlic and red onion and sauté until soft and lightly tanned.
8. Add the tomatoes with a pinch of salt and pepper and cook for 2-3 minutes until soft. Stir occasionally. If the pan is too dry you can add a table spoon of water.
9. Stir in the eggplant and walnuts. Keep cooking for another 5 minutes.
10. Remove from heat, add fresh parsley and stir.
11. Stuff the eggplant with the mixture.
12. Put back in the oven and bake for about 10 minutes.
13. In a large salad bowl place the rocket and cherry tomatoes.
14. Add a pinch of salt and pepper. Pour the olive oil, balsamic vinegar and lemon juice. Toss gently.
15. Serve the stuffed eggplant while still hot with the rocket salad on the side.

39. Stir-Fry Vermicelli with Vegetables and Tofu

Who doesn't love a good old stir-fry? We believe it is one of the quickest, healthiest and most delicious meals to prepare. By using bean threads (vermicelli), you will have a great low-carb dish that's also high in protein, thanks to the tofu. It is also full of vitamins and minerals, brought to you by a delectable selection of veggies.

Yield: 4 servings
Prep Time: 10 minutes
Cooking Time: 10-15 minutes

Ingredients:

- 2 x 3.5 oz. bean threads (Vermicelli)
- 14 oz. package firm tofu
- 1 large carrot – julienned
- 1 large courgette – julienned
- ½ white onion – sliced
- 5 cauliflower florets – chopped into smaller florets
- 5 broccoli florets - chopped into smaller florets
- 1 large green bell pepper – deseeded and sliced
- 1 handful of green beans – sliced
- 1 head bok choi – chopped
- 2 spring onions – finely sliced
- 2 cloves garlic – finely sliced
- 1 inch piece of ginger – finely sliced
- ½ chili – deseeded and finely chopped
- 2-3 tbsp. water

- 4 tbsp. tamari sauce
- ½ tsp. raw honey
- Juice of 2 limes
- ½ cup fresh coriander – roughly chopped
- Coconut oil
- Salt & Pepper

Preparation:

1. Soak the Vermicelli into cold water.
2. Drain the tofu and pat it dry with a paper towel.
3. Cut the tofu into bite size cubes and sprinkle with a pinch of salt and pepper
4. In a large wok or large frying pan heat 2 tablespoons of coconut oil over medium heat.
5. Fry the tofu until slightly golden and crispy on the outside, approximately 5 minutes.
6. Remove tofu from the wok and set aside.
7. Return wok to the stove and heat up 2 tablespoons of coconut oil over medium-high heat.
8. Add chili, ginger and garlic and stir-fry for 1 minute until golden brown. Be careful not to burn them.
9. Add vegetables except for bok choi and spring onion and stir-fry for approximately 2-3 minutes.
10. Add bok choi and spring onions. Stir-fry for another minute.
11. Drain the Vermicelli and cut them with a kitchen scissor or knife.
12. Add vermicelli to the wok and add water, tamari sauce, raw honey, lime juice and stir-fry for another minute.
13. Take off the heat, add tofu and fresh coriander.
14. Mix well and serve.

40. Broccoli and Zucchini Patties with Avocado and Walnut Salad

Why not to have a burger without a bun? This is a great substitute to a meat burger, and it will taste delicious together with a high-fat salad of avocado and nuts.

Yield: 4 servings
Prep Time: 20 minutes
Cooking Time 10-15 minutes

Ingredients:

- 1 large head of broccoli – stem removed and cut into florets
- 2 cups raw zucchini – peeled and chopped
- 2 tbsp. ground flaxseeds
- 2 tsp. Tamari sauce
- 1 tbsp. Dijon mustard
- 2 cloves garlic – minced
- Salt & Pepper
- 2 tbsp. whole-wheat breadcrumbs
- Extra virgin olive oil

For the Avocado Salad:

- 4 hearts Romaine lettuce – chopped
- 2 medium soft avocados – diced
- 1 cup cherry tomatoes – cut into halves
- ½ cup walnuts
- 1 tsp. grainy mustard

- 2 tbsp. extra virgin olive oil
- Juice of ½ lemon
- 1 tsp. balsamic vinegar
- Salt & Pepper

Preparation:

1. Preheat oven to 400F.
2. Line a baking tray with baking paper and place broccoli florets on top.
3. Drizzle with extra virgin olive oil and add a sprinkle of salt and pepper.
4. Toss well until evenly coated.
5. Put in the oven and bake for 15 minutes.
6. Take out of oven and late broccoli cool down.
7. When broccoli have cooled down place in a food processor together with the flax seeds, zucchini, Dijon mustard, salt and pepper.
8. Processes until all ingredients are well combined.
9. Add breadcrumbs and stir well with a spoon. Make 4 firm patties.
10. Put 2 tablespoons of extra virgin olive oil in a large frying pan over medium heat.
11. Cook your patties for approximately 5-6 minutes per side, until golden brown.
12. Set the patties aside on a paper towel and keep warm.
13. In a large bowl combine the Romaine lettuce, avocado, cherry tomatoes and walnuts.
14. In a small bowl whisk together grainy mustard, lemon juice, salt and pepper, balsamic vinegar and olive oil. Whisk until obtaining a creamy vinaigrette. If your vinaigrette is too thick you can dilute with couple drops

of water.

15. Pour the vinaigrette over salad and gently toss.
16. Serve the patties warm with avocado salad on the side.

DESSERTS

Healthy eating does not mean you have to give up on desserts all together. It just means that you should eat healthier desserts! Yes, desserts can indeed be healthy, and we can prove it with the following recipes. After all, a good meal needs a tasty conclusion to end in delight.

41. Quick Almond Butter Mousse

There is nothing more luscious than a creamy, velvety mousse. If you are a mousse lover, you cannot miss out on this quick-to-make, low-carb, high-fat mousse. It works as the perfect ending to a healthy meal, or simply as a treat anytime during the day. This mousse can also be frozen for an ice cream-like texture.

Yield: 4 servings
Prep Time: 10 minutes or less
Cooking Time: None

Ingredients:

- 2 x 13.5 oz. can full fat coconut milk – refrigerated overnight
- 4 tbsp. almond butter
- ½ tsp. liquid stevia
- ¼ cup almonds – chopped

Preparation:

1. Scoop the coconut cream at the top of the refrigerated cans of coconut milk into a bowl.
2. Add almond butter and stevia and whisk well. You can either use a manual or electric whisker.
3. Whisk until ingredients are well combined and you have a creamy fluffy mixture.
4. Pour the mousse into 4 small bowls.
5. You can serve immediately or put in the refrigerator to chill for approximately 1 hour. Alternatively you can freeze for approximately 30 minutes.
6. Top with chopped almonds before serving.

42. Strawberry Truffles

These creamy truffles will send you to heaven without feeling guilty about eating too much sugar. In fact, strawberries are very low in carbs, and if you choose a dark chocolate with a high cocoa content, it will contain a very minimal amount of sugar. Most of the calories will be from fat. It sounds just like the perfect combo for a vegan keto dessert!

Yield: 12 truffles
Prep Time: 15 minutes
Cooking Time: None
Firming Time: 45-60 minutes

Ingredients:

For the Filling:

- 1 cup strawberries – sliced
- 1 cup coconut butter
- 1 tsp. raw honey

For the Coating:

- 1 cup dark chocolate chips – choose a 70-80% cocoa content or higher
- 3 tbsp. almond milk

Preparation:

1. Put the filling ingredients in a food processor and mix

very well together.

2. The filling should have a soft but firm consistency. If it appears to be too soft, refrigerate for approximately 15 minutes.
3. Line a tray with a sheet of baking paper.
4. Spoon the mixture into 12 small balls onto the baking paper.
5. Put the balls in the freezer to firm up.
6. In the meantime melt the chocolate with the milk as follow:
7. Put milk and chocolate into a bowl.
8. Place the bowl on top of a saucepan with boiling water in it and stir until chocolate is completely melted, smooth and well combined with the milk.
9. Take the balls out of the freezer and roll them quickly one by one into the melted chocolate.
10. Place the balls back onto the baking paper and put them back in the freezer to firm up for approximately 45-60 minutes.

43. Avocado Chocolate Pudding

A healthy and delicious dessert that will leave your sweet tooth totally satisfied. Who would have ever thought that avocado and cocoa could taste so good together? This mouth-watering pudding is another winner in our list of low-carb, high-fat desserts.

Yield: 4 servings
Prep Time: 5 minutes
Cooking Time: None
Setting Time: 30 minutes

Ingredients:

- 2 large soft avocados – cut in half and pits removed
- 1 tsp. raw honey
- 1 tbsp. almond butter
- 2 tbsp. unsweetened cocoa powder
- ¼ cup dark chocolate chips (optional)

Preparation:

1. Place all ingredients into a food processor.
2. Process until obtaining a smooth and creamy mixture.
3. Divide the mixture into 4 small bowls.
4. Place in the fridge to set for at least 30 minutes.
5. Serve with a sprinkle of dark chocolate chips (optional).

44. Almond & Cocoa Mini Muffins

These mini muffins are very low carb since no flour is used. The regular sugar is replaced by coconut palm sugar, which is very low in fructose and therefore very suitable for a low carb diet.

Yield: 9 brownies
Prep Time: 10 minutes
Cooking Time: 18 minutes

Ingredients:

- ¼ cup coconut palm sugar
- 3 tbsp. water
- 1 vanilla pod
- 1 tbsp. almond oil (it can be substituted with another nut oil or olive oil)
- 1 cup almonds
- ¼ cup hemp seeds
- 2 tbsp. unsweetened coconut powder
- ½ tsp. baking powder
- ¼ tsp. baking soda
- ½ tsp. sea salt

Preparation:

1. Preheat oven to 350F.
2. Grease 9 mini muffin cups with some almond oil and dust with cocoa.

3. In a bowl mix coconut sugar, water, vanilla pod and almond oil.
4. Place almonds, hemp seeds, cocoa, baking powder, baking soda and salt into a food processor and process until you have a smooth powder.
5. Add the previously mixed wet ingredients and pulse for few seconds until combined.
6. Spoon the mixture into the mini muffin cups.
7. Bake in the oven for 15-18 minutes.
8. Remove muffins from oven and let them rest for 10 minutes.
9. Transfer muffins to a wire rack to cool.

45. Almond Butter Squares

You will be extremely pleased with these almond butter squares. The creamy almond butter mixed with coconut oil and chocolate makes it a delectable dessert.

Yield: 12 bars
Prep Time: 25 minutes
Cooking Time: None
Setting Time: 2 hours

Ingredients:

- 2 tbsp. coconut oil
- 1 cup and 2 tbsp. almond butter
- ¾ cup almond flour
- ¾ cup shredded coconut
- ¾ cup coconut palm sugar
- 4 ½ oz. dark chocolate 75% cocoa and over

Preparation:

1. Combine almond flour, shredded coconut and coconut sugar into a large bowl.
2. Melt 1 cup of almond butter and coconut oil over medium-low heat. If you want, you can melt it in the microwave for 15-30 seconds.
3. Once almond butter and coconut oil are melted, add to dry ingredients and mix well.
4. Take an 8"x 8" baking dish and press the mixture firmly

into it.

5. Place 2 tablespoons of almond butter and the chocolate into a small saucepan and melt over medium-low heat. Alternatively, you can place into a bowl and melt in the microwave for 30 seconds.
6. Pour the melted chocolate over the pressed mixture and smooth out the top with a knife.
7. Refrigerate for at least 2 hours until the mixture has set.
8. Cut into 12 squares and serve or keep refrigerated for later.

46. Coconut Whipped Cream

Yes, it is possible to make a vegan low-carb whipped cream, but still with a good amount of natural fat. You can enjoy this delicious whipped cream on its own, topped with dark chocolate chips, or to accompany any other dessert in this recipe book. Yum!

Yield: 2-3 cups
Prep Time: 15 minutes
Cooking Time: None

Ingredients:

- 2 x 15.33 oz. cans coconut milk – refrigerated overnight
- 2 tbsp. raw honey
- ½ vanilla pod

Preparation:

1. Scoop the solid coconut cream from the top of the cans and put into a bowl.
2. You can save the water for later and use it in smoothies or soups.
3. Place coconut cream, raw honey and vanilla pod into a mixer and beat on high speed for 10 minutes until firm and fluffy.
4. Serve the cream immediately, plain or topped up with dark chocolate chips.

47. Coconut Cookies

Really easy and quick to make, these coconut cookies can be enjoyed for dessert, but also for breakfast or an afternoon tea.

Yield: 8 cookies
Prep Time: 10 minutes
Cooking Time: 9 minutes

Ingredients:

- 3 tbsp. coconut flower
- 2 tbsp. coconut oil
- 1 tbsp. raw honey
- 1 pinch sea salt

Preparation:

1. Preheat oven to 365F.
2. Line a baking tray with baking paper.
3. Place all ingredients into a food processor and process until you have a soft and slightly sticky dough.
4. Divide the dough into 8 balls, place on the baking paper and flatten them slightly with the palm of your hand.
5. Put in the oven and bake for approximately 9 minutes until the edges are slightly tanned. Make sure you don't burn them.
6. Remove cookies from oven and let them cool completely before moving them to a serving plate.

48. Almond Macaroons

These delicious, almost bite-sized, macaroons with a touch of almond crunchiness and coconut oil goodness will be just the perfect low carb dessert to complete your healthy meal. The other advantage of this recipe is that no cooking is required.

Yield: 12 cookies
Prep Time: 15 minutes
Cooking Time: None
Chilling Time: 1-2 hours

Ingredients:

- 1 cup flaked or shredded coconut
- ½ cup sliced almonds
- ¼ cup macadamia nuts – chopped
- ¼ raw honey
- ¼ cup coconut oil – at room temperature
- ½ vanilla pod

Preparation:

1. Combine coconut flakes, almonds, and macadamia nuts into a mixing bowl and mix well together.
2. In a smaller bowl whisk together vanilla pod, raw honey and coconut oil.
3. Pour the whisked mixture over the coconut and nuts mix and stir well until all ingredients are combined to form a sticky and slightly stiff dough.
4. Divide the dough into two halves.

5. Put half of the dough into a food processor and pulse several times.
6. Puree for approximately 20-30 seconds until you have a smooth and soft paste.
7. Transfer the processed mix back with the other half and mix well.
8. Line a tray with baking paper.
9. Take the mixture and form 12 x 2" inch balls. Pack the balls tightly as you don't want them to crumble while you eat them.
10. Place the balls on the tray and press them slightly to flatten the bottom.
11. Chill in the refrigerator for 1-2 hours to allow them to set before serving.

49. Mixed Berry Mousse

This is the perfect dessert for a hot summer day. Quick and easy to make, this berry mousse will leave you feeling light and quenched.

Yield: 4 servings
Prep Time: 5 minutes
Cooking Time: None
Chilling Time: 30 minutes

Ingredients:

- 2 2/3 cups coconut milk
- 2 cups fresh mix berries (strawberries, raspberries, blueberries, blackberries, etc.) Frozen berries are also good if fresh ones are not available
- ¾ cup chia seeds
- 1 vanilla pod
- 2 tbsp. fresh lemon or lime juice
- 1 tsp raw honey

Preparation:

1. Put all ingredients in a blender and blend until smooth and creamy.
2. Pour the mixture into 4 glasses and refrigerate for approximately 30 minutes before serving.
3. Best served chilled.

50. Coconut Baits

These low carb baits will be the perfect answer to your sweet cravings. They are delicious consumed at room temperature or you can serve them frozen for that ice cream like texture.

Yield: 16 bites
Prep Time: 20 minutes
Cooking Time: None

Ingredients:

For the Filling:

- ½ cup coconut oil - softened
- 4 cups grated unsweetened coconut
- 3 tbsp. coconut nectar

For the Coating:

- 1 ½ cup dark chocolate chips
- 1 tbsp. coconut oil

Preparation:

1. Put the filling ingredients into a food processor and process for several minutes until you have a smooth mixture.
2. Line an 8"x 8" container with baking paper.
3. Spread the filling around the container.
4. Put the filling in the freezer for 15 minutes to solidify.
5. In the meantime, melt the chocolate together with the coconut oil. You can do this on the stove over low heat

or in the microwave for 30 seconds.

6. Take the filling out of the freezer.
7. Get the filling out of the container by lifting the baking paper.
8. Cut the filling into 12 bitesize pieces of any shape you like.
9. Line a tray with baking paper.
10. Dip the bites one by one into the melted chocolate and rest them on the tray.
11. But in the freezer to set for 5 minutes.
12. Serve or store into an airtight container in the fridge or freezer for later.

NIBBLES

Healthy nibbles can be enjoyed between meals, or when you suddenly get a little hungry. They are also great as pre-dinner appetizer before your main course, and they don't require much preparation.

51. Cucumber Bites

Fresh and delicious, these tasty cucumbers bites can really be enjoyed at any time of the day. Cucumber is low carb and refreshing; you will not feel guilty for nibbling away at these wonderful treats.

Yield: 14 bites approximately
Prep Time: 10 minutes (excluding soaking time)
Cooking Time: None
Soaking Time: 1-3 hours

Ingredients:

- 1 cup almonds – soaked 1-3 hours
- ¼ cup cashew nuts – soaked 1-3 hours
- Juice of 1 lemon
- 1 clove garlic –minced
- Salt & Pepper
- 1 tsp. olive oil
- 1 large cucumber – sliced into approximately 1 inch pieces
- 1 tomato – diced

- ½ cup fresh parsley – roughly chopped

Preparation:

1. Soak almonds and cashew nuts in warm water for 1-3 hours. The longer you soak them, the softer and creamier they will be.
2. Put all ingredients (except cucumber, parsley and tomato) into a blender or food processor.
3. Blend or process until you get a creamy paste.
4. If the mix is too thick for your likings you can add a little bit of water.
5. Remove the mixture from the blender.
6. Add the diced tomato and fresh parsley and gently mix with a spoon.
7. Scoop one spoonful of mixture onto each cucumber slice.
8. Sprinkle with black pepper and serve.

52. Broccoli Crispy Bread

This incredible vegan flatbread is low in carbohydrates, and contains fat from extra virgin olive oil. It is also enriched with protein from the chia seeds. You can enjoy this bread as a snack, or as an accompaniment to your meal.

Yield: 3-4 servings
Prep Time: 5 minutes
Cooking Time: 30 minutes

Ingredients:

- 4 cups of broccoli florets – cut into chunks
- 3 tbsp. nutritional yeast
- 1 tbsp. extra virgin olive oil
- 2 tbsp. chia seeds
- 1 tsp. baking powder
- Salt & Pepper
- ½ cup fresh basil

Preparation:

1. Preheat oven to 375F.
2. Soak the chia seeds with 6 tablespoons of water for about 5 minutes.
3. Put broccoli into a food processor and pulse until you get a texture similar to rice.
4. Add nutritional yeast, basil, salt and pepper, and pulse until ingredients are well combined.

5. Transfer the mix into a bowl, add olive oil, baking powder, chia seeds and stir well.
6. Line a baking tray with a sheet of baking paper.
7. Pour the dough onto the baking paper and spread evenly. The thinner you make it, the crispier it will be.
8. Bake in the oven for approximately 30 minute until golden and crispy. Make sure it is cooked in the middle.
9. Remove from the oven and cut into bars.
10. Enjoy while still warm or cold.

53. Roasted Pumpkin Seeds

Roasted pumpkin seeds are simply awesome to nibble on, or to add to your soups or salads. They are a great source of magnesium and zinc, and one of the best sources of plant-based omega-3s.

Yield: as much as you like
Prep Time: 5 minutes
Cooking Time: 25 minutes

Ingredients:

- Pumpkin Seeds
- Extra virgin olive oil
- Salt & Pepper

Preparation:

1. Preheat oven to 350F.
2. Line a baking tray with baking paper or aluminium foil. Either will do.
3. Place the seeds into a bowl, drizzle with not too much oil but enough to evenly coat them.
4. Sprinkle with salt and pepper and toss well together.
5. Pour the seeds onto the baking tray and roast in the oven for approximately 20 minutes or until they become very lightly brown. Keep an eye on them not to burn them.
6. During cooking remove the tray a few times to stir the seeds.

7. When completely roasted, remove from oven and let them cool.
8. Enjoy as nibbles or sprinkle on your salad or soup.

54. Multi Seeds Crackers

These super healthy crackers are perfect to enjoy plain, or with the dip of your choice. They are delicious, crispy and full of good fats and protein provided by the different types of seeds.

Yield: 20-30 crackers depending on the size you cut them
Prep Time: 10 minutes
Cooking Time: 1 hour

Ingredients:

- ½ cup chia seeds
- ½ cup sunflower seeds
- ½ cup pumpkin seeds
- ½ cup sesame seeds
- 1 cup water
- 1 large clove garlic or 2 small – minced
- Salt & Pepper

Preparation:

1. Preheat oven to 300F.
2. Put all seeds into a large bowl and add water. Stir well until combined.
3. Let the seeds rest for 3-5 minutes until the chia seeds absorb the water.
4. Stir again. There should be no more water on the bottom of the bowl.
5. Use a spatula to spread the mixture onto the baking

paper. Spread into two rectangles approximately 12"x 7" in size and approximately 1/8 to ¼ inch thick.

6. Sprinkle with salt and pepper.
7. Bake in the oven for 35 minutes.
8. Remove from oven and turn the rectangles around very carefully with a spatula.
9. Put back in the oven and back for another 25-35 minutes.
10. Keep an eye on them to make sure they don't burn.
11. Remove from oven when the edges are lightly golden.
12. Set aside to cool down for approximately 10 minutes.
13. Break the rectangles into crackers and let to cool completely.
14. You can store these crackers in an airtight container for up to 1 month, but we honestly think they will not last you that long as they are too moreish!

55. Almond Cauliflower

This one is perfect to taste as a nibble and appetizer. It can also be a great choice of side to one of your main dishes.

Yield: 4 servings
Prep Time: 5 minutes
Cooking Time: 30 minutes

Ingredients:

- 4 cups cauliflower florets – chopped into bite size chunks
- 1 tbsp. extra virgin olive oil
- 2 tbsp. almonds – chopped in very small pieces

Preparation:

1. Preheat oven to 425F.
2. Line a baking tray with baking paper.
3. Place cauliflower into a bowl, add olive oil, salt and pepper, almonds and toss everything well together.
4. Pour the cauliflower onto the baking paper.
5. Bake in oven for approximately 30 minutes or until golden brown and soft. Stir occasionally.
6. Remove from oven, sprinkle with ground black pepper and serve.

SAUCES & DRESSINGS

In this section, you will find some sauces and dressings that can be used to add a final touch to your mains and salads.

56. Tahini Dressing

This dressing is not only delicious and versatile, but it is also full of healthy properties thanks to the tahini paste. Tahini is made out of sesame seeds, which are an excellent source of copper, omega-3 and omega-6.

Yield: 4-6 servings
Prep Time: 5 minutes
Cooking Time: None

Ingredients:

- ¼ cup tahini paste
- Juice of 1 lemon
- 1 tbsp. apple cider vinegar
- 2 tbsp. extra virgin olive oil
- 2 clove of garlic – minced
- Salt & Pepper

Preparation:

1. Place all ingredients into a blender (except for water).
2. Blend until creamy.

3. If the dressing is too thick, add a little bit of water until it reaches the desired consistency.

57. Lemon & Mustard Vinaigrette

This is an all-time favorite, it goes well on any salad, and it is both keto and vegan friendly.

Yield: 6 tablespoons
Prep Time: 5 minutes
Cooking Time: None

Ingredients:

- Juice of 1 lemon
- ½ tsp. Dijon mustard
- 4 tbsp. extra virgin olive oil
- Salt & Pepper

Preparation:

1. Put lemon juice, mustard, salt and pepper into a bowl.
2. Whisk well until combined.
3. While whisking, drizzle in the extra virgin olive oil.
4. Keep whisking vigorously until all ingredients are combined and you have a medium creamy dressing.
5. The dressing should be ready at this point. You can taste and adjust any of the ingredients to taste.

58. Cheesy Sauce

This vegan cheesy sauce is rich in taste and texture. It works great as a topping for roast veggies or vegan burger patties.

Yield: 4 servings
Prep Time: 5 minutes
Cooking Time: None

Ingredients:

- 2 tbsp. extra virgin olive oil
- 2 tbsp. nutritional yeast
- Juice of 1 lemon
- Salt & Pepper

Preparation:

1. Combine all ingredients together into a bowl and whisk vigorously.
2. Serve as an accompaniment to your dishes.

59. Chimichurri Style Sauce

This sauce is a combination of great flavors and herbs, very similar to the Argentinian Chimichurri. You can drizzle this on top of your veggies, salads and even soups. You can even use it as a dip! You can make a big batch of this and store it in the fridge.

Yield: 2/3 cup
Prep Time:
Cooking Time: 5 minutes

Ingredients:

- ½ cup extra virgin olive oil
- 1 tsp. fresh rosemary
- 1 tsp. fresh oregano
- 2 medium cloves garlic – crushed
- 2 tsp. smoked paprika
- 1 bay leaf
- ¼ tsp. sea salt
- 1 tbsp. lemon juice
- Pinch of black pepper flakes

Preparation:

1. Put the herbs into a mortar and pestle and lightly pound them. If you do not have a mortar and pestle you can chop them very finely.
2. Pour olive oil into a pan and warm over medium-low

heat.

3. When oil is hot, remove from heat.
4. Stir paprika, black pepper flakes, bay leaf and a pinch of salt into the oil.
5. Add herbs and lemon juice.
6. Put the sauce into a jar in the fridge and leave it to infuse for a couple of days before using.

60. Peanut Sauce

This very popular Asian sauce will be a winner with your Asian and non-Asian dishes alike.

Yield: 1 cup
Prep Time: 10 minutes
Cooking Time: 5 minutes

Ingredients:

- ½ cup creamy peanut butter
- 2 tbsp. Thai red curry paste
- ¾ cup coconut milk
- 2tbsp. apple cider vinegar
- 1/2 tbsp. coconut palm sugar
- 2 tbsp. ground peanuts
- Salt

Preparation:

1. Add all ingredients together into a saucepan and whisk well.
2. Transfer the pan to the stove and heat up the mix over a low heat while continuing whisking.
3. Keep a constant eye on the sauce and as soon as it starts bubbling remove from heat. If you like the sauce more liquid, add a little bit of water and whisk. Keep adding water bit by bit until it reaches your desired consistency.
4. Move the sauce into a bowl and top with ground peanuts.

DIPS & SPREADS

Despite common beliefs, dips can be incredibly healthy, and can be consumed as part of a ketogenic vegan diet. The dips we propose here mainly include nuts (which are very high in natural fat and proteins), avocado (which are also very high in monounsaturated fatty acids), and low carb vegetables.

61. Spicy Almond & Garlic Dip

This hummus-like creamy dip is delicious with raw vegetables or crackers. It is very easy and quick to make, and you can keep it in the refrigerator for 3-4 days.

Yield: 1 large cup
Prep Time: 5 minutes
Cooking Time: None
Soaking Time: overnight

Ingredients:

- 1 cup raw almonds – soaked overnight
- 1 cup almond milk
- 2 cloves garlic
- ½ tsp. chili powder
- ¼ tsp. smoked paprika
- Pinch of salt
- Pinch of Cayenne pepper

Preparation:

1. Put all ingredients into a blender.
2. Blend until smooth and creamy.
3. You can use immediately or refrigerate covered.

62. Cauliflower Hummus

You do not have to give up hummus to stick to your low carb diet. With this great recipe that substitutes chick peas with low carb cauliflower, you will still be able to enjoy a tasty hummus. It goes great with any kind of raw vegetable.

Yield: 2 cups
Prep Time: 5 minutes
Cooking Time: 5 minutes

Ingredients:

- 4 cups cauliflower stems and florets – chopped
- 2 tbsp. tahini paste
- 5 tbsp. extra virgin olive oil
- Juice of 2 lemons
- Salt & Pepper
- Pinch of cumin

Preparation:

1. Steam or lightly boil cauliflower for approximately 5 minutes or until soft.
2. Drain and let it cool down completely.
3. Combine cauliflower, tahini paste, extra virgin olive oil, lemon juice and cumin into a food processor. Process until creamy. Alternatively, you can use a blender.
4. Add salt and pepper to taste.
5. You might want to taste it and add more lemon juice or

olive oil according to taste.

6. Serve with raw vegetables.

63. Eggplant & Walnut Spread

Eggplant together with walnuts is a winning combination. If you mix these two, you will surely enjoy a delicious ketogenic vegan appetizer that you can use as a spread or dip according to your likings.

Yield: 1 large cup
Prep Time:
Cooking Time: 45

Ingredients:

- 2 x medium round eggplants
- 1 tbsp. extra virgin olive oil
- 1 cup walnuts – chopped
- 2 cloves garlic
- Juice of 1 large lemon
- Salt & Pepper
- 1 tsp. cumin
- 1/3 cup Tahini paste
- ½ cup fresh parsley leaves

Preparation:

1. Preheat oven to 375F.
2. Place eggplants on a baking tray and rub them with the olive oil.
3. Stab them with a knife a couple times.
4. Roast for 45 minutes until they look deflated and

wrinkled.

5. In the meantime toast the walnuts in a pan over medium-high heat for 3-4 minutes. Leave to cool

6. When eggplant is cooked, remove from oven and let it cool down.

7. Cut the eggplants in half and scoop the flesh out into a food processor.

8. Add walnuts and all other ingredients. Process until obtaining a paste.

9. Serve into a bowl with a drizzle of extra virgin olive oil accompanied by crackers or raw vegetables.

64. Coconut Yogurt Dip

You'll find a mix of creamy goodness in this coconut yogurt dip, enriched with garlic, cucumber and tangy lemon juice.

Yield: 2 cups
Prep Time: 10 minutes
Cooking Time: None

Ingredients:

- 1 ½ cup coconut yogurt
- 1 large cucumber – peeled and cut into chunks
- 3 cloves garlic
- Juice of 1 lemon
- 2 tbsp. extra virgin olive oil
- ½ cup fresh coriander – finely chopped
- Salt & Pepper

Preparation:

1. Place all ingredients (except coriander) into a blender and blend until smooth.
2. Add salt and pepper to taste and the coriander.
3. Mix well with a spoon.
4. Refrigerate for about 1 hour to let the flavours infuse.
5. Stir the dip well before serving.

65. Olive Tapenade

A classic spread with all the goodness of olives and olive oil that can be made in almost no time.

Yield: 1 cup
Prep Time: 5 minutes
Cooking Time: None

Ingredients:

- ½ cup black olives
- ½ cup green olives
- 2 cloves garlic
- 1tsp. lemon juice
- Ground black pepper

Preparation:

1. Put all ingredients together into a food processor and process for few seconds. You basically want all ingredients finely chopped and well mixed together. Be careful not processes for too long otherwise you will have a paste.
2. Serve to spread onto your favourite crackers.

66. Chunky Rocket Spread

This super healthy tangy spread can be shared as an appetizer with crackers, or you could use it to make canapes for a special dinner.

Yield: 1 cup
Prep Time: 15 minutes
Cooking Time: None

Ingredients:

- 1 ½ cup roasted Cashew nuts
- 1 clove garlic
- 3 cups rocket leaves
- ¼ cup nutritional yeast
- ¼ cup extra virgin olive oil
- Juice of ½ lemon
- Salt & Pepper

Preparation:

1. Place the Cashew nuts, garlic and nutritional yeast into a food processor.
2. Pulse gently until the nuts are still chunky and mixed well together with the other ingredients.
3. Transfer the mix into a bowl.
4. Place olive oil and lemon juice into the food processor, then add rocket leaves and pulse to blend.
5. Transfer the rocket mixture into the bowl with the

Cashews, season with salt and pepper and mix together with a spoon.

6. Serve with crackers or other low carb breads.

SMOOTHIES & SHAKES

A fresh smoothie or shake is always a great healthy treat. Whether you want to quench your thirst, or if you simply want a quick breakfast or snack during the day, we have the perfect combination of healthy ingredients you can use to stick to your ketogenic vegan diet.

67. Avocado & Raspberry Smoothie

This is a delicious and healthy combination for a creamy smoothie. Raspberries have many health benefits, including helping with weight loss and boosting the immune system. You combine it with the fatty acids, vitamins and minerals of avocado, and you will have a winning drink.

Yield: 2 servings
Prep Time: 2 minutes
Cooking Time: None

Ingredients:

- 1 ripe avocado – cut in half, pit and skin removed
- 1 cup water
- 1/3 cup coconut milk
- ½ cup fresh raspberries (you can use frozen if fresh are not available)
- 2 ice cubes (optional)

Procedure:

1. Add all ingredients into a blender.
2. Blend until smooth and creamy.
3. Serve in a glass.

68. Strawberry Coconut Smoothie

This must be the ultimate vegan keto smoothie. Incredibly quick to make! We've included high-fat ingredients, such as coconut milk and almond butter, to give your low-carb strawberry drink some nice thickness.

Yield: 2 servings
Prep Time: 2 minutes
Cooking Time: None

Ingredients:

- 1 cup fresh strawberries
- 1 cup unsweetened coconut milk
- 2 tbsp. almond butter
- 2 ice cubes (optional)

Preparation:

1. Pour all ingredients into a blender.
2. Blend until smooth and creamy.
3. Serve in your favourite glass.

69. Thai Style Coconut Shake

This is a great shake for those sizzling summer days. Close your eyes while drinking it, and you could see yourself on a tropical beach in Thailand. Savour the goodness of coconut!

Yield: 2 servings
Prep Time: 2 minutes
Cooking Time: None

Ingredients:

- 2 cans full fat coconut milk
- Ice cubes

Preparation:

1. Pour coconut milk and 5-6 into a blender
2. Blend until ice is crushed.
3. Check thickness of your shake. The more ice you add, the thicker your shake will be.
4. Keep adding ice until you reach desired thickness.
5. Serve immediately into a tall glass garnished with an orchid flower (optional).

70. Frozen Berry Shake

This is another summer-day shake, perfect when you feel like an ice cream. You can choose any low carb berries, depending what is available.

Yield: 2 servings
Prep Time: 2 minutes
Cooking Time: None

Ingredients:

- 1 cup coconut cream
- 1 cup almond milk
- 1 cup mixed fresh berries (strawberries, raspberries, blueberries, depending what is available) – you can substitute with frozen berries if fresh are not available
- 2 cups ice

Preparation:

- Place all the ingredients into a blender.
- Blend until smooth and frozen.
- Serve immediately.